Easy Holiday & Seasonal
Art Projects With Paper

BY JO LYNN ALCORN

SCHOLASTIC
PROFESSIONAL BOOKS

NEW YORK • TORONTO • LONDON • AUCKLAND • SYDNEY
MEXICO CITY • NEW DELHI • HONG KONG

For Antonio, Cynthia, and Elisa,
for all their help

Front cover and interior design by Kathy Massaro
Cover art by Jo Lynn Alcorn
Cover photos by Donnelly Marks
Interior illustrations by Jo Lynn Alcorn except pages 5 and 6 by Paige Billin-Frye
Interior photos by Johnny Alcorn

ISBN: 0-590-43371-7

Contents

Introduction 4
How to Use This Book 5
Helpful Hints About Paper and Paint 6

Fall Fun

Frisky Fall Squirrel 12
Autumn Leaves & More 14
Going Batty 17
Perky Turkey 19
Pilgrim Storage Canisters 21

Winter Wonders

Jolly Snowman 24
Dear Deer Notepad 27
Kwanzaa Mat (Mkeka) 29
New Year's Noisemaker 32
Groundhog Pop-Up Card 34
Valentine Keeper 36
Chinese New Year Dragon 38
Shamrock Pop-Up Card 41

Spring Things

Festive Flowers 43
Spring Flowers Vase 46
Happy Earth Day Card 48
Quilt a Card 51
Mini Bunny Piñata 54

Summer Celebrations

Ladybug, Ladybug 57
Flutter-By Butterfly 59
Bookworm Bookmark and Reading Log 62
Fancy Fans 64
Summertime Journals 66

Collages for All Seasons 69
Pattern Pages 71

*W*hat do the seasons, paper, and children have in common? Aside from their natural beauty, they are all full of surprises! This book uses the seasons as a source of inspiration for art projects made with paper. The seasons provide a natural division to the school year, each season having its own holidays, rhythms, and colors that children respond to naturally. Children will delight in creating projects like the Frisky Fall Squirrel, Perky Turkey, Jolly Snowman, and the Flutter-By Butterfly. These artful creations can be used to decorate your classroom and by children to share as gifts with friends and family on special occasions throughout the year.

To make these unique projects, children will use essentially one material: paper. Paper is one of the simplest, most basic, and available materials. Yet in my work as a paper collage artist, I am continually amazed at the virtually endless possibilities for using this material—the paper in a pad, flat and uniform, becomes transformed when cut, bent, folded, fringed, curled, crimped, or woven into a beautiful flower, a dragon, or other fanciful creations. A flat piece of paper is just one color, but as light hits a piece of paper that has been folded, the two planes appear in light and shadow, creating the illusion of two colors. With the projects in this book, children will discover and explore the many possibilities and qualities of this versatile material.

Besides being creative art experiences, these projects connect naturally with science, social studies, reading, language arts, and other subjects. You may, for example, want to take your class on a nature walk in the fall to observe the changing palette of autumn leaves before settling in to create them in your classroom. The Chinese New Year Dragon provides a perfect opportunity for reading books about Chinese culture, customs, and traditions. Related classroom activities, projects, and books to read accompany many of the projects. Each classroom-tested project also includes complete, easy-to-follow directions, diagrams, and helpful tips.

Please feel free to use these ideas as taking-off points for you and your students. Encourage invention and innovation, and don't be afraid to make changes or try new things! And above all, have fun!

—*Jo Lynn Alcorn*

How to Use This Book

Each project in this book takes you from preparation to finished project. Here's an overview of what you'll find:

Materials
A complete list of all materials and equipment needed for the project as well as possible substitutions.

Reproducible Patterns
Easy-to-cut-out patterns are included for some of the projects. Children can simply cut out the pattern box, tape it to a piece of construction paper, then cut out the shape inside the pattern box. This way, it is not necessary for children to cut out the more detailed shape more than once.

Steps
Step-by-step instructions take you through each project, along with helpful tips to make the process go smoothly.

Variations
Here you'll find suggestions for simplifying or altering the basic project as well as ways to add enhancements.

Ways to Display
From bulletin board ideas to dioramas, unique and inviting ideas for showcasing students' creations, plus additional activities that integrate the project with other curriculum areas.

Book Breaks
Suggested fiction and nonfiction books and related activities that connect with the holiday or seasonal project.

Tips for Managing the Projects

- For ease and efficiency, it's always a good idea to give children the supplies they will need in the most ready state possible. While many of the projects use standard 9- by 12-inch construction paper, others use paper that has been cut to certain sizes (to avoid waste). Consider stocking a Supply Station (a table or bookcase will work nicely) with packets of needed materials that get passed out on the day of the project. If space is limited, you can even create a Supply Station on a bulletin board.

- Tack up envelopes of different sizes to hold precut papers.

 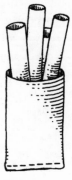

- Paper cups or boxes, such as milk cartons, make greater holders for crayons, markers, and scissors. Use pushpins or staples to attach them to the board.

Make handy pockets to hold a variety of tools by stitching or stapling acetate to a strip of cardboard, as shown. Or use resealable sandwich bags and staple them side by side to the board.

All the projects in this book can be made using the simplest materials most commonly available in classrooms. Occasionally, students will need materials that are easily brought from home, such as coffee cans with plastic lids for the Pilgrim Storage Canisters (page 21). Review the list of materials a week or two before you start each project, and ask students to bring in any needed materials ahead of time.

Try to test the art projects before doing them with children. This will help you to identify needed materials, familiarize yourself with the steps, and assess the amount of time you'll need, including time for preparation, setup, and cleanup. It's also helpful to have a finished model on hand to serve as inspiration!

When you begin, make a new project along with children to illustrate how each stage will look. Take one step at a time and wait for the class or group to proceed with you. Later on, you might set up projects at stations to encourage children to explore on their own.

Helpful Hints About Paper and Paint

Read this section before you begin the projects with your students. Here you'll find simple directions for basic paper folding and cutting techniques that will be used in many of the projects. Also included are simple techniques for using paint in unusual ways to enhance the projects. Encourage children to use the painting and paper techniques they learn in this book to come up with ideas for their own projects.

A Word About Paper

The projects in this book can be made with standard size construction paper (9 by 12 inches and 12 by 18 inches), but almost any kind of sturdy paper can be used as long as it is neither too heavy, making cutting difficult, nor too lightweight, making the product too flimsy.

Heavier papers or even cardboard (from used file folders or cereal boxes, or shirt cardboard from a dry cleaners) can be used to strengthen projects as backing sheets, and lightweight papers (such as crepe and tissue paper) are useful for decorative touches or collage.

Brown paper bags are a versatile, available, and sturdy source of paper, and they look great painted or worked on with crayons and markers. "Found" papers such as magazine pages, wrapping paper, product labels, and newspapers are magnificent sources of inspiration for collage. Aluminum foil is unique for its shiny quality. In short, if it works, use it!

About Cutting

It's important to have good, reasonably sharp, left-hand/right-hand safety scissors with pointed ends. These are easy to find, inexpensive, and intended for use by children five years and older. Good scissors make snipping a snap!

Most of the techniques used in this book are sufficiently simple—cutting, gluing, stapling, taping, folding, bending—that they will hardly need any explanation. The rest are just as easy, but perhaps not as familiar, so they are listed and explained below along with some general tips to use in the classroom.

Cutting on the Fold

Half patterns are given for the projects. They are placed against the folded edge of a piece of folded paper and are then cut out, beginning the cut at the fold.

Folded edge

Cutting Fringe

Hair can be made by cutting parallel slits in paper.

Folding

Most of the folding in this book involves folding a piece of paper in half by lining up the corners and creasing the fold. Using a thumb or the side of a ruler to press the fold makes a cleaner, crisper fold.

Folding on Dotted Lines

Dotted lines in the patterns show where to fold the paper after it has been cut.

Accordion Folds

In this technique, paper is folded back and forth in ridges that form "mountains" and "valleys." This technique is used for the Perky Turkey, Chinese New Year Dragon, the Bookworm Bookmark, and the Fancy Fans.

Curling

To give flat pieces of paper a curled shape, roll them around large markers, pencils, or any other curved object. Use this technique to enhance the Festive Flowers project (page 43).

Crimping

To crimp paper, make a slit and then overlap the two parts and glue or tape them together. Crimping is used to make the Frisky Fall Squirrel (page 12).

Scoring

To score a piece of paper, "draw" a line on paper pressing firmly with an old, empty ballpoint pen. This makes a dent in the paper that serves as a guideline for folding. This works well for making curved and irregular folds, a wonderful way to make flower petals and leaves look more alive.

Some Handy Tools and Materials for Decorating

- A hole punch is useful in almost any project. It's great for punching holes that can serve as eyes, nostrils, spots on a ladybug, or polka dots, as well as for making holes to use with paper fasteners or yarn.

- Hole reinforcements, which come in bright colors, make dandy eyes or lovely decorations such as spots on the Flutter-By Butterfly (page 59).

- Pipe cleaners make wonderful flower stems and legs for animals or can be twisted into a colorful broom for the Jolly Snowman (page 24).

- Craft yarn has a variety of uses—as a handle for the Valentine Keeper (page 36), the pulls on the Mini Bunny Piñata (page 54), and the Perky Turkey's wattle (page 19), to name just a few.

- Markers, crayons, colored pencils, and paint can be used to decorate projects and create features such as eyes, noses, and mouths.

About Paint

Painting is an important and rewarding experience for children in the early grades. They thrive on the uninhibited, tactile quality of painting and the world of creative expression it opens up for them. Many of the projects in this book will be enhanced by having students first paint and pattern the papers they will be using. Construction paper, though durable and suitable, comes in a limited range of colors; painting is a wonderful way for children to personalize their work.

Children will enjoy exploring the following painting and patterning techniques to create unusual and unique effects. (Painting can, of course, be messy. To minimize mess, have children make a handy Paint Station (see page 10) that will contain drips and splashes on painting occasions.)

Spattering

Materials:

- poster paint
- plastic cup or dish
- old toothbrush
- construction paper
- scrap of cardboard

1 Pour a small amount of paint into the plastic cup or dish. Dab the toothbrush lightly in the paint, picking up paint on the tips of the bristles.

2 Hold the toothbrush over the construction paper and angle it down toward the paper. Drag the scrap of cardboard against the bristles from far tip to near tip. The paint will scatter in interesting splatters and blobs. (It's easier to do this with a finger than cardboard, but messier!)

Stenciling

Materials:

- scraps of paper (for making stencils)
- white or light-colored construction paper
- poster paint
- plastic cup or dish
- old toothbrush
- scrap of cardboard

1 Make stencils by cutting different shapes out of paper scraps. Place these on white or light-colored paper.

2 Using the spattering technique (see left), cover all areas around the stencils with paint. When the paint is dry, remove the stencils. Repeat this process as many times as desired. This simple technique creates both striking and subtle results.

Sponging

Materials:

- kitchen sponge
- scissors
- water
- plastic cup or dish
- poster paint
- construction paper

1 Cut a dry kitchen sponge into small, simple shapes such as squares, circles, diamonds, triangles, stars, and so on. (Note: You can substitute precut sponge shapes available at craft stores.)

2 Moisten the sponge shapes, wringing out excess water.

3 Pour a small amount of paint into the plastic cup or dish. Then dab a sponge shape lightly in the paint (only a little paint is needed; too much will clog up the pores of the sponges, which create interesting textures). Press the painted surface of the sponge against the paper. Refill the sponge with paint as needed.

Stamping

Materials:

- ◎ poster paint
- ◎ plastic cup
- ◎ construction paper
- ◎ chopsticks, corks, straws, and other materials that can be used as stamps

Gather various materials to use as stamps. Dip the end of a chopstick into paint to create great polka dots. Make larger circles with a cork. Use them together to make animal tracks. The possibilities are endless!

Combing

Materials:

- ◎ fingerpaint paper or other coated paper
- ◎ poster paint
- ◎ plastic cup
- ◎ paintbrush
- ◎ plastic fork or comb
- ◎ paper towels

1 Pour a small amount of paint into the cup. Paint a large area of the paper with poster paint. (Use a color that contrasts well with the paper.)

2 Draw the fork or comb firmly across the painted surface while it is still wet. This pushes aside the paint to expose the color of the

paper underneath. By moving the fork or comb as you go along, you can make wavy lines or zigzags.

You can also use the fork or comb as a drawing tool. Simply dip the tool into paint and then draw it across a piece of paper.

Blotting or "Pulling Off"

Materials:

- ◎ construction paper
- ◎ poster paint
- ◎ plastic cups
- ◎ paintbrushes

1 Fold a piece of construction paper in half, then open it up again.

2 Pour a small amount of paint into a plastic cup. Use a separate cup and fresh brush for each color. Using one color at a time, paint a pattern on one half of the paper. Apply the paint generously but not too thickly (drying time increases with thicker paint).

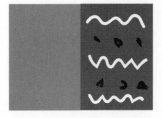

3 After applying each layer of color, and while the paint is still wet, close the paper and rub gently over it, then pull it open slowly. It's not necessary to wait for each color to dry before adding another, and children may add as many layers of paint as they like. This technique (used in the eighteenth century to create wallpaper patterns), creates a soft, feathery effect.

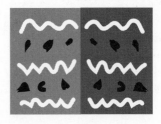

How to Make a Paint Station

From my work in classrooms, I know that many teachers are reluctant to begin the "messy business" of setting up and cleaning up after painting. This simple-to-make "paint station" will help greatly. Children will be better able to organize themselves and focus on the fun at hand if they have a special place to work freely. For easy management and space constraints, I suggest making a few of these and letting children take turns at the stations.

Materials (for each station):

- large corrugated cardboard box with top flaps
- box cutter or X-acto knife (adult use only)
- 4 plastic cups or dishes
- paper towel tube
- two 3-inch hook-and-loop adhesive strips (Velcro)
- tape
- scissors
- paper towels, cut into quarters (to avoid waste and make them more manageable)
- old, oversized shirts (to be used as smocks)

1 Position the box so that the wider end faces you. Use a box cutter (adult only) to cut open one side of the box as shown. Flatten the cut side

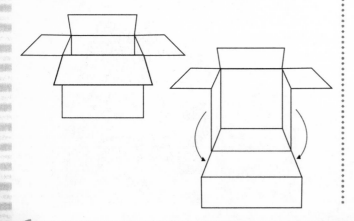

on a table or desk. This becomes part of the work surface. The top and side flaps become handy ledges to lay wet painted papers on.

2 Set four plastic cups against the back wall of the box. Three of these are for paint and one is for water for cleaning brushes.

3 Cut the cardboard tube in half. Place the two halves vertically against the back wall of the box (or against the sides if there is no more room) and tape in place. These make handy holders for brushes and other patterning tools such as old toothbrushes, chopsticks, plastic forks, combs, and so on.

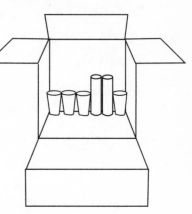

4 Close the box back up and close the flaps. Cut one Velcro strip in half. Remove the backing and attach each half to either side of the flaps as shown. Don't remove the backing from the second strip of Velcro; this adheres to the two short strips on the flap, keeping them closed. When the day's painting is done, students close the box back up, using it as storage for their supplies, papers, and scraps. Invite children to decorate the outside of the Paint Station.

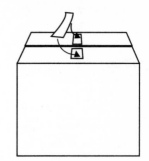

Painting Tips

- Have children wear smocks when working at the station. Also, have plenty of paper towels on hand.

- Fill the paint and water cups. Limit children to three different colors of paint and the amount of paint to about one quarter of the plastic cup. Children don't need 10 colors to produce beautiful paintings—in fact it may confuse them. The three primary colors (red, yellow, and blue) produce a range of other colors. Give children refills on paint if necessary, but always encourage them to use their supplies with care.

◎ Messier techniques such as spattering with a toothbrush can be done toward the back of the Paint Station so that any drips, splatters, or spills will be caught by the three walls.

◎ When painting papers for projects in this book, you will sometimes want to do the painting and the project as two separate sessions, especially if the paint has been applied very heavily. Paint needs time to dry, though poster paints dry very quickly. A good plan might be to have children take turns painting papers right before lunch or recess so that they are ready to be worked with upon return.

◎ Encourage children always to wash brushes after using and blot on a paper towel. Store brushes with bristles up.

◎ At the end of a painting session, have children rinse out the cups and return them to the Paint Station.

Make a Scrap Saver

Don't throw away that scrap paper! That little piece of red paper may be the eye of a dragon, or a volcano erupting, or… That green scrap with zigzags could be grass, or the hair of a monster, or… That yellow piece might become the sun, or a flower…. As children cut and snip away creating the projects in this book, there will be lots of leftover bits and pieces of paper. Encourage children to think of these scraps as precious supplies to be stored for future uses in collages or for decorating other projects. Not only does this teach them to be resourceful and not wasteful but it also stretches their imagination to see fantastic possibilities in ordinary scraps of paper. Here's how to make a Scrap Saver, a handy storage place for these odds and ends.

Materials (for each child):

◎ one 9- by 12-inch piece of construction paper
◎ scraps of paper for decorating
◎ glue stick
◎ scissors
◎ stapler

1 Fold the paper in half and staple together the sides.

2 Decorate by cutting out shapes from the paper scraps and gluing onto the folder. Have children write their names on the folder, or, for a fun challenge, invite them to cut their names out of paper.

3 Remind children to use their Scrap Saver for all their paper scraps. They're going to be doing a lot of snipping and cutting!

On page 69 you'll find a special section called Collages for All Seasons. So, if the Scrap Savers get a little full, maybe it's time to do a collage!

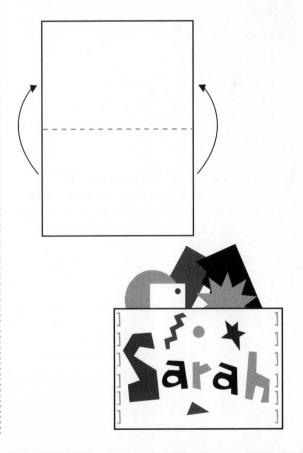

Frisky Fall Squirrel

Squirrels are a common sight in the autumn as they scurry around gathering their nuts for the winter. This three-dimensional squirrel, perfect for an autumn art project, can even hold an acorn in its paws!

Materials

For each student:

- squirrel patterns (pages 71–72)
- 2 pieces of 9- by 12-inch brown construction paper

Other materials:

- tape
- scissors
- markers or crayons
- hole punch (optional)

Copy and hand out the squirrel pattern pages to each child. Have children cut out the boxes around the squirrel's body, tail, and head. Then show children how to do the following steps.

1 Fold one piece of construction paper in half the long way. Fold the other piece in half the short way.

2 Line up the pattern boxes along the folded side of the construction paper as shown, and tape them to the paper to hold them in place while cutting.

3 Cut out the shapes of the body, tail, and head on the outer solid lines, cutting through all layers of the paper and tape. Then fold the ears, arms, and legs inward along the dotted lines. Remove the patterns.

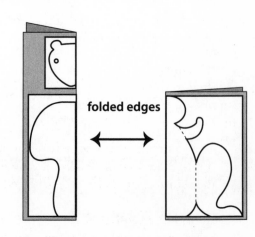

folded edges

4 Open up the tail. Starting at the top, cut down along the fold about 2 inches, then close up the tail again.

5 Line up the folded side of the body with the folded side of the tail and tape them together as shown. Tape up to where the slit in the tail begins. Turn the squirrel over and tape the tail to the body on the other side. Open up the tail and body and adjust the squirrel until it stands up.

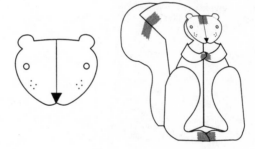

6 Overlap the two sections of the tail at the slit to form a rounded tail shape. (This is called crimping.) Fasten with tape.

7 Draw a nose, eyes, and whiskers on the squirrel's face. Use tape to attach the face to the squirrel's body, letting it flap open at the bottom. When you tap on the squirrel's nose, it will bob up and down in a very squirrelish way!

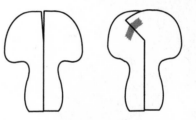

8 Join together the feet with tape. Do the same thing with the arms.

◎ Now make acorns and autumn leaves for the squirrel's nest. Turn to page 14 to find out how to make them.

Variations

◎ The squirrel makes a nifty hand puppet. Have children slip a hand up through the feet and hook their fingers over the arms. Now they can make the squirrel nod its head, scurry, and hop!

◎ Instead of a squirrel, invite children to adapt the basic patterns to make other animals such as a rabbit, mouse, dog, or cat.

Tip

For a different effect, use a hole punch to make the squirrel's eyes instead of drawing them and glue on pieces of straw from a broom for whiskers! For a finishing touch, cut out two white construction paper teeth and tape them to the face from the back.

Book Break

Children will be fascinated by the close-up photos of squirrels, birds, and other animals that live on and inside a maple tree in Bianca Lavies' *Tree Trunk Traffic* (Dutton, 1989).

13

Autumn Leaves & More

There is nothing that says autumn more than a blanket of rustling red, brown, rust, orange, and yellow leaves on the ground. Invite children to create their own paper leaves, acorns, and pinecones to bring this colorful season indoors.

Materials

- ⊚ autumn leaf, acorn, and pinecone patterns (page 73)
- ⊚ 6-inch squares of construction paper in fall colors (red, yellow, orange, and so on, for leaves)
- ⊚ 6-inch squares of brown construction paper (for pinecones)
- ⊚ scraps of ochre, green, or light brown paper (for acorns)
- ⊚ tape
- ⊚ scissors
- ⊚ markers or crayons

Getting Ready

Prepare children for this project by taking a nature walk in the fall to observe the changing colors of leaves and the textures of acorns and pinecones. (If you live in an area that doesn't experience the changing colors of leaves, show children pictures of trees with leaves that have turned color. See Book Break, page 16.) Ask children to observe and describe the colors they see (green, multicolored, red, brown, rust, and so on). Encourage them to incorporate their observations into their projects as they create and decorate them.

Copy and hand out the pattern pages to each child. Have children cut out the boxes around each shape. Then demonstrate the following steps.

1 Fold the pieces of construction paper in half. Line up the pattern boxes along the folded sides of the paper as shown, and tape the patterns to the paper to hold them in place while cutting.

2 Cut out the shapes of the leaves, pinecone, and acorn along the outer solid lines. Remove the oak leaf pattern.

3 Fold the maple leaf along the dotted line. Then remove the pattern.

4 Remove the pinecone pattern and draw a crosshatch pattern on it, if desired.

5 Fold the acorn down on the bottom dotted line, and back up on the top dotted line. Remove the pattern and draw a crosshatch pattern on the cap of the acorn.

Book Break

Colorful, detailed, and bright, the close-up photos of thirteen different autumn leaves seem to pop off the pages in Ken Robbin's glorious book *Autumn Leaves* (Scholastic, 1998).

The National Audubon Society Pocket Guide: Familiar Trees of North America (Knopf, 1996) and Arthur Dorros's *A Tree Is Growing* (Scholastic, 1997) are both excellent references for identifying different kinds of leaves.

Share *Why Do Leaves Change Color?* by Betsy Maestro (HarperCollins, 1994), a book that explains, in simple terms, the reason for the beautiful leaf colors we see each autumn.

Variations

◎ Point out to children that the leaves that are on the ground are not always flat—sometimes they are folded and even crumpled. Encourage children to use the following techniques to make their leaves even more realistic: Score the leaves with an old, empty ballpoint pen, and then fold them back along the drawn lines. (See page 7 for more on scoring.) Or try crumpling the paper and then opening it back up.

◎ This project would be an excellent occasion for a painting party before the students cut out their leaves. Use the spattering technique on page 8 to create subtle and rich effects that will look simply gorgeous!

◎ Though leaf patterns have been provided for maple and oak leaves, children can cut out their own leaf shapes, using real leaves as models or tracing them onto paper. Or show children pictures of different leaf shapes.

Ways to Display

◎ Let children landscape a tabletop with an autumn display. If children also make the Frisky Fall Squirrel (see page 12), they can glue or tape the acorn to the squirrel's paws, then surround their furry friend with autumn leaves, which the squirrel will need to keep its nest warm all winter long! Place books with information about autumnal changes around the display to invite reading. (See Book Break, left, for suggestions.)

◎ Punch a hole through one end of each of the leaves, pinecones, and acorns, and string them across the classroom. Or tape these colorful mementos of fall to classroom windows.

Going Batty

A lways a favorite at Halloween time, this simple yet lifelike paper bat hangs right-side-up or upside-down and can flap its wings!

Materials

For each student:

◎ bat patterns (page 74)
◎ 9- by 12-inch piece of black construction paper
◎ 12-inch black or brown pipe cleaner (the large, fuzzy kind is best)

Other materials:

◎ tape
◎ scissors
◎ hole punch
◎ light-colored paper scraps (optional)

Pass out all the materials. Have students cut out the bat pattern box. Then demonstrate the following steps.

1 Fold the black construction paper in half the long way. Line up the pattern box along the folded side of the construction paper as shown. Tape the pattern to the paper in a few places to hold it in place.

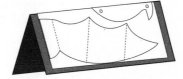

2 Punch holes through the dots on the bat's body. Then cut out the bat's wings and body. Cut through all layers of the paper.

3 Remove the patterns. Tape together the two sections of wings as shown.

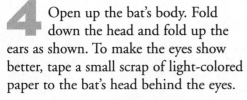

4 Open up the bat's body. Fold down the head and fold up the ears as shown. To make the eyes show better, tape a small scrap of light-colored paper to the bat's head behind the eyes.

5 Tape the wings to the back of the bat's head.

6 Fold the pipe cleaner in half. Slip the ends through the punched holes in the bat's body. Tape the folded pipe cleaner to the back of the wings, leaving a loop at the top for a fingerhold or hanger. Fold up the ends of the pipe cleaner to form feet.

7 Fold back the wings close to the bat's body.

8 Turn the bat over so that it is facing you. Now fold each wing inward in two places as shown. Each wing should have three folds in all.

Children can hold their bat by its pipe cleaner loop and make it make dip and soar with wings flapping or sleep upside-down with folded wings! (To do this, simply fold back the pipe cleaner loop and find a quiet spot to hang it.)

Ways to Display

While this lifelike bat will provide children with plenty of October fun, it can also provide a basis for learning about this fascinating mammal. Create a "Going Batty" display by hanging children's creations over a bookshelf filled with books about bats. (See Book Break, left.)

Perky Turkey!

Let children get involved in planning for their family's Thanksgiving celebration. This adorable turkey makes a pleasing centerpiece for the table. Or children can make a turkey to perch at each plate, welcoming family members and friends to their seats. Either way, this project will invite children to talk with their families about the meaning and traditions of Thanksgiving.

Materials

For each student:

◎ turkey pattern (page 75)

◎ two 9- by 12-inch sheets of construction paper (brown, yellow, or orange; use two different colors, one for the tail feathers and the other for the body)

◎ 12-inch pipe cleaner (the fuzzy kind works best)

◎ 4-inch length of red yarn

Other materials:

◎ tape

◎ scissors

◎ hole punch

◎ crayons or markers

◎ stapler

Pass out the supplies, including copies of the turkey pattern box. Then show children how to do the following steps.

1 Make the turkey's body: Fold one of sheet of paper in half the short way. Line up the turkey pattern box along the folded side of the paper as shown, and tape the pattern to the paper to hold it in place while cutting.

2 Cut out the shape of the turkey along the outer solid lines, cutting through all layers of paper and tape.

3 Punch a hole in the beak where indicated in the pattern.

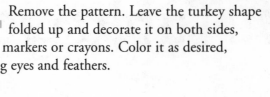

Book Break

Celebrate the funny and offbeat aspects of Thanksgiving with poems like "Gobble Gobble" and "If Turkeys Thought" in Jack Prelutsky's whimsical collection *It's Thanksgiving* (Greenwillow, 1982).

For a realistic look at wild turkeys, share Jim Arnosky's *All About Turkeys* (Scholastic, 1998). From wattles to gobbles, this lively-written book is packed with interesting facts about these fascinating creatures.

4 Remove the pattern. Leave the turkey shape folded up and decorate it on both sides, using markers or crayons. Color it as desired, adding eyes and feathers.

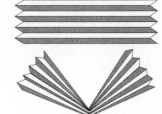

5 Make the tail feathers. Fold the other sheet of paper back and forth along the long edge to make accordion folds about 1 inch wide. Now fold this folded paper in half to create the fan shape of the turkey's tail feathers.

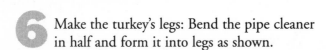

6 Make the turkey's legs: Bend the pipe cleaner in half and form it into legs as shown.

7 Put the turkey together: Place the turkey's body inside the fan shape as shown. Then put the ends of the pipe cleaner on either side of the turkey's body, between the body and the tail fan. Staple all parts together at the base of the fan. This may take some help from the teacher or an adult; if you gather the parts carefully, it should take only one staple.

8 Now for the finishing touch—the turkey's wattle! Thread the red yarn through both holes in the turkey's beak and let it hang down evenly. Now we're talking turkey!

Variations

Invite children to adapt the basic design to create other kinds of birds such as ducks, flamingos, peacocks, or fantastic imaginary birds.

Ways to Display

To make your gobbler stand up, push its legs underneath the rim of a plate. If you push its head down lightly it will bob back and forth as if it were pecking at the food on the plate! Consider adding some colorful autumn leaves (see page 14) to make the table even more festive. Happy Thanksgiving!

Pilgrim Storage Canisters

The first Thanksgiving was a celebration of the Pilgrim's first successful harvest. This meant that they would have food to store away for the long winter ahead. Children will enjoy making these Pilgrim storage canisters to hold everything from candies to crayons.

Pilgrim Girl

For each student:

◎ empty 11-ounce coffee can with lid (with no sharp edges)
◎ 5- by 13-inch piece of construction paper (to cover can)
◎ construction paper in contrasting colors (for hair and face)
◎ 9- by 12-inch piece of white construction paper (for hat)

Pilgrim Boy

For each student:

◎ two empty 11-ounce coffee cans with lids (with no sharp edges)
◎ paper plate (an inch or two larger than the coffee can)
◎ two 5- by 13-inch pieces of black construction paper (to cover cans)
◎ construction paper in contrasting colors (for hair and face)
◎ black, white, and yellow construction paper (for hat)

Other materials:

◎ tape
◎ scissors
◎ paper scraps
◎ markers, crayons, colored pencils, paints and brushes
◎ glue stick and liquid glue

Tip

A few weeks before doing the activity, ask children to bring in empty coffee cans from home. You may wish to precut construction paper to the specified dimensions for children. (See page 5 for more.)

Instructions for the girl and boy Pilgrims are the same except for the hats. Show students how to follow these steps.

1 Wrap a piece of 5- by 13-inch construction paper around the can, taping it closed where it overlaps. (For the Pilgrim boy, fasten black paper around both cans.) Check that the lids will still fit on the cans. If not, trim a little from the top of the paper so that it doesn't touch the lid.

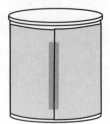

2 Cut out a face to fit on the can, and draw features with crayons or other decorating supplies. Use a glue stick to attach the Pilgrim's face to the can.

3 Make the hair: Fold the paper for the hair lengthwise as shown. Cut fringe through both layers of the paper to about 1 inch from the edge. Then unfold the paper.

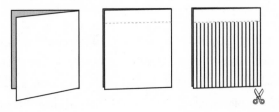

4 Apply glue above the fringe and attach the hair to the can. To customize the hairdo, curl the paper fringe, give the hair a trim, or attach bangs cut from paper scraps.

Pilgrim Boy's Hat

1 Place the paper plate on a piece of black construction paper, trace around it, and cut out the circle. This large circle is the hat brim.

2 Center the second can on the hat brim, then trace around it. Remove the can and put a wide bead of glue all along the traced line. Set the can back in place and let dry.

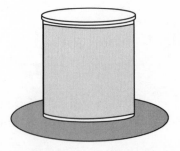

22

3 Make a hat band by taping a long strip of white paper around the base of the hat.

4 Make a buckle by drawing a small square on a square piece of yellow paper. Glue the buckle to the hat brim. (Just one spot of glue in the middle of the buckle is enough—the buckle looks better if it's not flat.)

5 Set the hat can on top of the face can and you have a Pilgrim boy who looks like he's saying "Hats off to you!"

Pilgrim Girl's Hat

1 Using a 9- by 12-inch piece of white construction paper, fold over about 2 1/2 inches as shown.

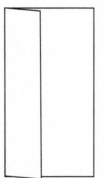

2 Fold the paper in half and tape together at the edge as shown.

3 Open up the hat and place it over the can, flattening it as much as possible on top and folding it down over the rim as shown. Now the Pilgrim girl has a smart, starched hat!

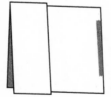
Variations

Challenge children to think of ways they could adapt these projects to make a Wampanoag Indian girl or boy.

Book Break

Read aloud or have children read books that relate the story of the Pilgrims and the first Thanksgiving. For a fascinating look at a day in the life of Pilgrim and Wampanoag children, share *Sara Morton's Day*, *Samuel Eaton's Day*, and *Tapenum's Day*— all by Kate Waters and published by Scholastic.

Jolly Snowman

Here's a snowman that children can make, whether or not there's snow on the ground! For this project, let children work in groups, with each group making one stand-up snowman that will make a whimsical, wintry tabletop centerpiece.

Materials

For each snowman:

- snowman patterns (page 76)
- white bond paper
    - two 5- by 17-inch strips
    - one 4- by 17-inch strip
    - one 2- by 11-inch strip
    - one 11-inch square
- tape
- scissors
- pipe cleaners (2 white, 1 yellow, and 3 black)
- black construction paper
- colorful crepe paper streamers
- wiggle eyes (optional)
- scraps of colored paper
- markers
- glue

Pass out the materials, including the patterns. Have children cut out the pattern boxes. Then demonstrate how to do the following steps.

Making the Snowman's Body

1 Tape together the two 5- by 17-inch strips, end to end. Tape the largest pattern box (the snowman's base) to strip of paper as shown.

2 Starting at the pattern end of the strip, fold the paper back and forth, making accordion pleats as wide as the pattern.

3 Firmly press together the folds with the pattern on top. Then cut out the pattern along the outer solid lines, cutting through all layers of paper. Remove the pattern.

4 Continue to hold the stack as you tape together the straight edges of the folds, making sure to catch all of the edges with tape.

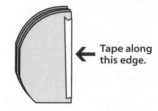

← Tape along this edge.

5 Follow steps 1 to 4 for the snowman's middle and head.

Assembling the Snowman

1 Open up the snowman's base so that it forms a circle, with the taped seam running down the middle. Twist together the two white pipe cleaners and place them against the seam as shown. Tape securely in place.

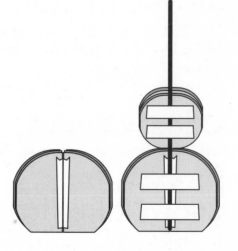

2 Do the same thing with the middle section, placing it above the base.

3 Next, wrap a black pipe cleaner once around the white pipe cleaners, right above the snowman's middle. These will be the snowman's arms. Twist small pieces of pipe cleaner around the end of each arm to form hands.

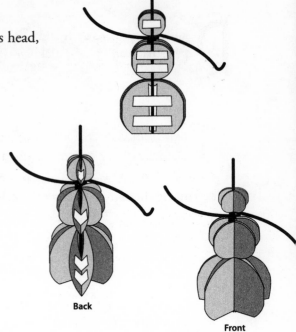

4 Repeat step 1 with the snowman's head, placing it right above the arms.

5 To make the snowman stand up, begin with the base and pull together the top layers of the folds on either side of the pipe cleaners. This will create a sphere. Tape or glue together. Do the same thing with the middle and the head.

Back

Front

6 Arrange the folds of each section so that they are spaced evenly and the snowman stands up. Shape the arms, bending up the hands.

7 Give the snowman a face by drawing on eyes or gluing on wiggle eyes. Make a carrot nose from orange construction paper and attach to the head. Other finishing touches follow.

Broom

Use a yellow and black pipe cleaner to make a broom for the snowman to hold.

Stovepipe Hat

Cut a circle out of black construction paper for the brim. Make a small slit in the middle. Then slide it down over the white pipe cleaner on top of the snowman's head. For the stovepipe, make a tube out of a rectangular piece of black paper. Tape or glue it at the seam. Tape or glue the stovepipe to the hat brim.

Cheery Scarf

Wrap a strip of brightly colored crepe paper around the snowman's neck. (Fringe the ends, if you like.)

Snowflake Base

Cut a circle out of the 11-inch square of bond paper. Fold the circle into thirds and make cuts as shown.

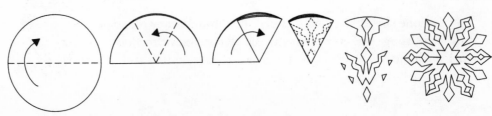

Dear Deer Notepad

The winter holidays are definitely the season for making lists and checking them twice. Here's a wonderful early winter project—a reindeer notepad that students can take home to their families before the holidays or make as gifts for stocking stuffers.

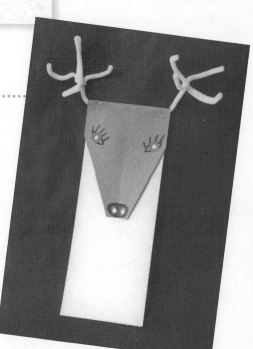

Materials

For each student:

- deer head pattern (page 76)
- 5- by 12-inch piece of brown construction paper
- a stack of ten to fifteen sheets of 4 1/4- by 11-inch bond paper (cut standard 8 1/2- by 11-inch paper in half)
- 3 pipe cleaners (the fuzzy kind works best)

Other materials:

- tape
- scissors
- crayons or markers
- hole punch
- stapler

Pass out the materials. Have students cut out the deer head pattern box. Then show children how to do the following steps.

1 Fold the brown construction paper in half as shown. Line up the pattern box along the folded side of the construction paper. Tape it to the paper to hold it in place.

2 Cut out the deer's head, cutting right through all layers of the paper. Then remove the pattern.

3 On one side of the folded paper, draw the deer's eyes and nose using markers or crayons. Make nostrils with a hole punch.

4 Insert a pipe cleaner under the fold of the deer's head and center it. Also insert the stack of papers and staple across the top so that both the pipe cleaner and the papers are held tightly.

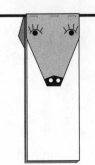

5 Bend up each end of the pipe cleaner to form antlers.

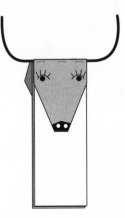

6 Bend the other two pipe cleaners in half. Wrap them around the antlers as shown. Shape them to form "branches" on the main antlers.

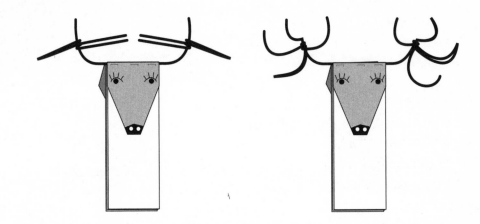

Variations

Children may want to use their imagination to create notepads for other holidays—for example, Bunny-Ear Notepads for Easter or Butterfly-Topped Notepads for summer!

Kwanzaa Mat (Mkeka)

Kwanzaa, a celebration of African American heritage, begins on December 26 and ends on January 1. Based on African harvest customs, this ceremony involves placing various symbolic items on a woven straw mat, called an mkeka (em-KAY-kah).

In this project, children begin by patterning papers with poster paints, using a pull-off technique, then weaving them into an mkeka. The interplay of colors and patterns creates a rich textural effect, reminiscent of African textiles.

For each student:

- two 9- by 12-inch pieces of black, orange, or pink construction paper
- poster paints (red, green, and yellow) and brushes
- 1-inch-wide ruler
- scissors
- glue stick

Painting the Papers

Begin by having children paint their papers. They will need three colors—red, green, and yellow. Guide children through the following process.

1 Fold the two pieces of construction paper in half. Then open them up again.

Tip

Check your library for books that show examples of African art—textiles in particular. Invite children to incorporate aspects of these designs into their mats.

Tip

Painting and blotting should be done quickly, while the paint is still wet. It's not necessary to wait for each color to dry before applying another. Children may also add as many layers of paint as they like.

2 Using one color at a time, paint a pattern on one half of the piece of paper. Designs might include stripes, circles, dots, zigzags, triangles, sun shapes, waves, and so on. Paint should be generous but not goopy, as drying time increases with thicker paint.

3 After applying each color, close the paper and rub gently over it, then pull open slowly. This pull-off technique creates a soft, feathery, and interesting pattern. Allow the painted papers to dry.

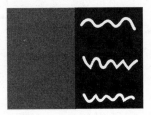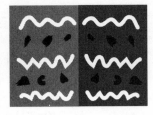

Weaving the Mats

1 Position one of the pieces of paper horizontally. Use a 1-inch-wide ruler to mark off 9 strips. Then cut out these strips.

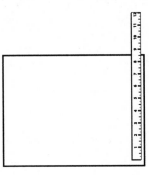

2 Fold the other piece of paper in half the short way. Starting at the fold, and 1 inch from one side, cut a straight, zigzag, or wavy line through the paper to about 1 inch from the open edge of the paper.

3 Repeat this process to make 6 more slits, each about 1 inch apart. (You can first measure and draw lines about 1 inch apart if you like.)

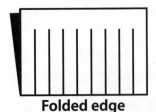

Folded edge

30

4 Open the paper and spread it flat. Weave the strips into the slits by slipping each strip over and under them. If you begin with the first strip over the background, start the second strip underneath. Continue weaving strips until you have filled the paper. Push the strips close together as you work. Then glue the edges of the strips in place.

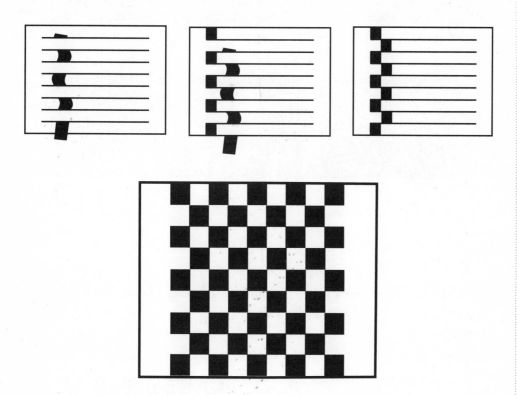

Book Break

Share The Gifts of Kwanzaa by Synthia Saint James (Albert Whitman, 1994) to introduce children to this African American holiday. Bright, bold graphics accompany the simple text that explains the *Nguzo Saba* (the Seven Principles) and the meaning of various rituals and symbolic objects.

Another good book is *K Is for Kwanzaa* by Juwanda G. Ford (Scholastic, 1997), an alphabet book in which each letter of the alphabet introduces a term or fact about Kwanzaa.

Ways to Display

Ask students if they celebrate any special holidays or traditions in the winter. Are there special symbols like the mkeka for their holiday? Invite children to bring them to class and discuss the meaning and importance of each symbol. Designate a table where students can display their mkekas along with other objects they bring in to share.

New Year's Noisemaker

*S*hake, rattle, and ring in the New Year with these delightful and decorative noisemakers!

Materials

For each student:

- paper towel tube
- bright, colorful construction paper (about 6 by 11 inches)
- twelve 1-foot lengths of assorted colored yarns
- two 4-inch squares of fabric (an old sheet will work well)
- 2 rubber bands

Other materials:

- poster paints and brushes
- hole punch
- hole reinforcements (colored if possible)
- tape
- an assortment of dried foods in paper cups (rice, popcorn kernels, beans, small nuts in their shells, berries, broken pieces of spaghetti or other pasta)

1 Pass out the materials except for the dried foods. Let students choose a piece of colored construction paper.

2 Have students paint their paper with bright, colorful patterns.

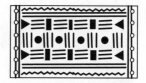

3 When their papers are dry, have students punch six evenly spaced holes along each short side of the paper. They can reinforce the holes with colored hole reinforcements, if desired.

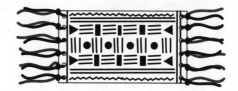

4 Next, students thread the pieces of yarn through the holes and knot them.

5 Set the cups filled with the dried foods on a table. Let children take turns choosing materials with which to fill their noisemakers. To make an interesting sound, encourage them to use objects of different sizes, from very small (rice) to large (lima beans). Then show them how to do the following steps:

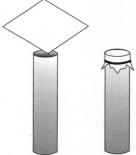

- Place a square of fabric over one end of the cardboard tube. Stretch it over the tube and fasten tightly with a rubber band. Make sure there are no holes or gaps in the fabric. Trim off any excess.

- Turn the tube over and add a handful of different noisemaking materials.

- Now close the tube, repeating the step with the other fabric square and rubber band.

- Wrap the painted paper tightly around the tube, keeping the pieces of yarn pulled out of the way. Tape along the seam where the paper overlaps. Now shake, shake, shake!

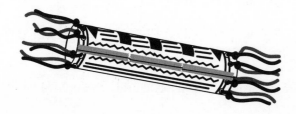

Groundhog Pop-Up Card

As spring approaches, everyone looks forward to seeing what the groundhog will do. Will it come out of its burrow and see its shadow or not? Here is a fun and easy pop-up card that children will love to make and play with.

Materials

For each student:

- ◎ groundhog pattern (page 74)
- ◎ 4-inch square of brown construction paper (for groundhog)
- ◎ 9- by 12-inch piece of contrasting construction paper (for card)
- ◎ two 1- by 3 1/2-inch strips of paper (same color as card)

Other materials:

- ◎ scissors
- ◎ tape
- ◎ markers and crayons

Pass out the materials and a copy of the pattern box to each child. Then model for children how to do the following steps.

1 Fold the brown construction paper in half. Line up the groundhog pattern box along the folded side of the paper and tape in place.

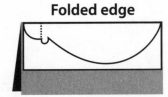
Folded edge

2 Cut out the groundhog shape, cutting through all layers of the paper.

3 Open up the groundhog's body and fold the head down along the dotted line. Then remove the pattern. Draw in eyes, a nose, and paws with markers or crayons.

Book Break

The Story of Punxsutawney Phil, the Fearless Forecaster by Julia Spencer (Crown, 1977). How reliable is a groundhog's weather prediction? Read this appealing story to find out!

4 Tape the two strips of paper to the bottom of the groundhog, one in front and one in back, as shown. Fold up the strips.

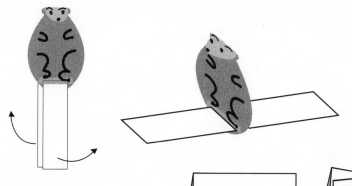

5 Fold the paper for the card in half the short way. Then fold it in half again.

6 Open up the folded card. Line up the groundhog with its strips along the bottom open edge of the card. Place the groundhog with its strips flat on the card as shown.

7 Tape the strips to the card, with the tape angled over the corners as shown. Fold back the strips at an angle along the edges of tape. When the card is closed, the groundhog will peek over the top, and go back inside when the card is opened.

8 Decorate the front of the card with markers and crayons.

MR. GROUNDHOG says it's SPRING!

Ways to Display

Make these cards before Groundhog Day, and have students record their predictions about whether or not the groundhog will see its shadow when it comes out of its burrow. Make a two-column graph on a bulletin board. Title one column "Groundhog Will See Its Shadow" and the other "Groundhog Won't See Its Shadow." Let children tack up their card in their chosen column. Then wait for Groundhog Day and compare their predictions with the actual "results"!

Valentine Keeper

Roses are red, violets are blue, here's an adorable Valentine's Day project to do! Children will love making this nifty holder to tuck away the valentines they receive.

Materials

For each student:

- ◎ heart pattern (page 77)
- ◎ one 12- by 18-inch piece of red or pink construction paper
- ◎ one yard of red or pink yarn

Other materials:

- ◎ tape
- ◎ scissors
- ◎ hole punch
- ◎ crayons or markers
- ◎ paper doilies, glitter, sequins, stickers (optional)

Pass out the materials including copies of the valentine pattern page. Have children cut out the pattern box. Then show children how to do the following steps.

1 Fold the sheet of construction paper in half twice as shown.

2 Line up the pattern box along the folded side of the construction paper and use tape to hold the pattern in place.

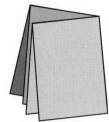

3 Cut out the heart shape along the outer edge, cutting through all layers of paper.

4 Use the hole punch to make holes as indicated on the pattern.

5 Remove the pattern and unfold the paper. You will have two hearts.

6 Weave the piece of yarn in and out of the holes around the heart. Then pull the ends of the yarn so they meet at the top of the hearts as shown.

7 Tie a knot about halfway down, then tie in a bow.

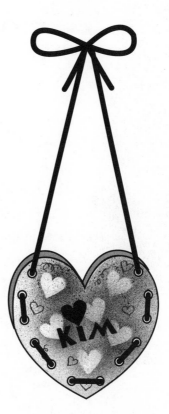

8 Have children print their names on the hearts and decorate with a variety of materials such as glitter, sequins, bits of paper doilies, stickers, or shapes cut from paper scraps. Students may also enjoy using different painting techniques such as spattering or stenciling (see page 8).

Ways to Display

In advance of Valentine's Day, create a Valentine's Day bulletin board display. Let children use pushpins to hang up their Valentine Keepers. Then invite secret and not-so-secret valentines to deliver their messages, cards, and notes to their classmates' Valentine Keepers.

Tip

If students want to use paint to decorate their Valentine Keeper, have them do this before they weave in the yarn.

Book Break

Children will be inspired to write their own valentine poems when you share the enchanting poems and jingles in *Good Morning to You, Valentine* edited by Lee Bennett Hopkins (Boyds Mills Press, 1993).

Also share Jean Marzollo's *Valentine Cats* (Scholastic, 1996), a charming story that is a perfect complement to students' art projects. The cats in this story busily make and decorate valentine cards for friends and family.

Chinese New Year's Dragon

An exciting and colorful festival, the Chinese New Year is usually celebrated in February according to the Chinese calendar. Giant dragon floats are paraded through the streets to bring good luck in the new year. The dragon is a symbol of health and prosperity. In this project, children make their own New Year's dragons. Use them to hold your own parade around the classroom!

Materials

For each student:

◎ dragon head pattern (page 75)

◎ two 4- by 18-inch strips of brightly colored construction paper (for dragon's body)

◎ one 4 1/2-inch square of construction paper (for dragon's head)

◎ one 4- by 9-inch strip of construction paper (a different color for the tail)

◎ scraps of colored paper

◎ one 12-inch red pipe cleaner (for dragon's tongue, or use a strip of red paper)

◎ 2 chopsticks or rulers (optional)

Other materials:

◎ tape

◎ scissors

◎ glue stick

◎ hole punch

◎ colored or white hole reinforcements for eyes and nostrils

◎ markers and crayons

Pass out the materials. Have children cut out the dragon head pattern box and then set it aside. Show children how to do the following.

1 Starting at the end of one of the long strips of paper, make a fold about one inch deep. Now fold the paper back another inch in the opposite direction. Keep folding back and forth until you have folded the entire piece of paper. This is called an accordion pleat. Now do the same thing with the other long strip of paper.

2 Glue together the two body pieces so that they form one continuous back-and-forth pleat. Set the body aside.

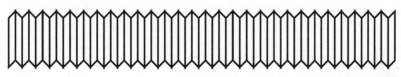

3 Fold the square of paper for the head in half. Line up the pattern box along the folded side of the paper as shown, and tape it down in a few places.

4 Cut out the head shape along the outer edges, cutting through all layers of paper. Use the hole punch to make nostrils and fold up on the dotted line.

5 Remove the pattern and spread open the dragon's head. Add hole reinforcements to the nostrils if desired.

6 Cut out two large circles for the eyes. (Stack two pieces of paper and cut out two at a time for symmetrical eyes.) Draw eyes on the circles or use hole reinforcements. Glue these to the head so that they stick out over the top of the head. Bend up in the same direction as the nostrils.

7 Cut out fringe for whiskers and glue these underneath the dragon's head. Cut out a shape for a top comb and glue it to the head between the eyes. Let it stick up over the top of the head like hair.

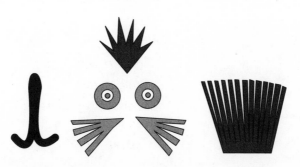

Tip
To make the dragons even more colorful, paint the papers ahead of time. See page 8 for more.

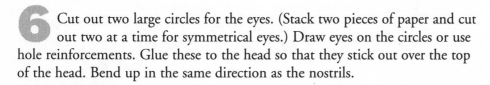

Book Break

Share *Lion Dancer: Ernie Wan's Chinese New Year* by Kate Waters (Scholastic, 1990), the true story of a Chinese boy looking forward to his first performance in a Chinese New Year parade on the streets of New York City. After sharing this story, let your students use their paper dragons in their own Chinese New Year parade.

Then invite your class to find about the Chinese New Year and its many customs. According to Chinese tradition, each year in a 12-year cycle is named after an animal— rat, buffalo, tiger, rabbit, dragon, snake, horse, goat, monkey, rooster, dog, and pig. Help children to find out what animal sign they were born under.

8 Fold the pipe cleaner in half and curl the ends outward to make the dragon's tongue. Tape it under the head. Or, instead, use a long, thin strip of red paper for the tongue and write a lucky fortune on it. Glue the end under the dragon's head. Then roll it up and friends can unroll the tongue to see what the dragon is saying.

9 Glue the head to the body.

10 Fringe the piece of paper for the tail and glue it to the end of the body. Now the dragon is ready to roar!

🌀 Optional: Attach chopsticks or rulers to the dragon's head and tail with tape. These can serve as handles for holding the dragon up high in a parade.

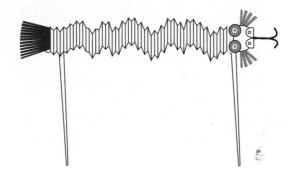

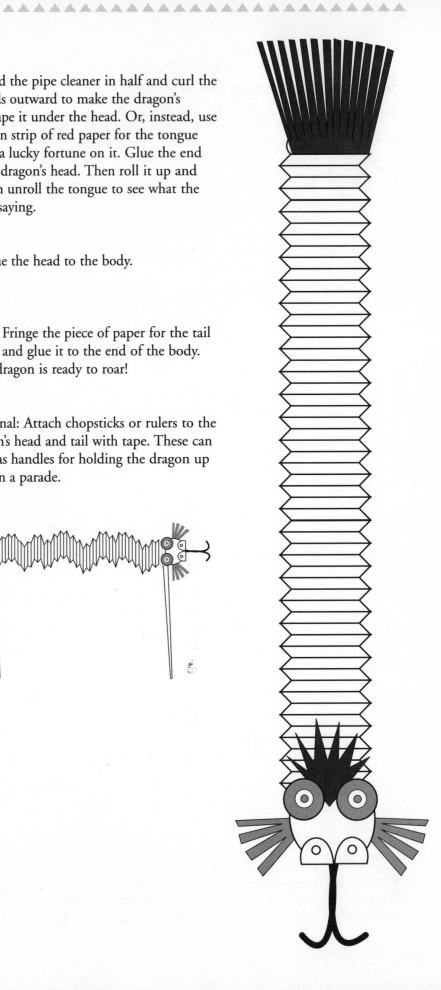

Shamrock Pop-Up Card

I t's the luck of the Irish! Here's another fun and easy pop-up—this one for St. Patrick's Day.

Materials

For each student:

◎ one 9-inch square of green construction paper (for clover)

◎ one 6- by 9-inch piece of construction paper in a contrasting color (for card)

Other materials:

◎ scissors

◎ glue stick

◎ markers and crayons, paint, or glitter

Pass out the materials. Then show children how to do the following steps.

1 Fold the green construction paper in half the long way as shown. Then fold it in half again the short way. Finally, fold it in half one more time along the diagonal as shown.

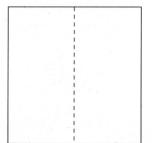

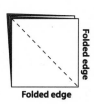

2 Holding the paper by one corner between the two folded edges, cut a curve that goes from one folded edge to the other. (Imagine you are holding an ice cream cone and what you are cutting out is the mound of ice cream on top).

3 Open up the paper—you will have a symmetrical four-leaf clover.

4 Push the opposite sides of the clover inward, and close it up to form a heart shape as shown.

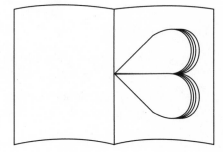

5 Fold the other piece of construction paper in half the short way. Then open it up. Apply glue to one side of the heart shape. Place it glue side down on the card as shown.

6 Then apply glue to the other side of the heart shape and close up the card. Let the glue dry. When you open up the card, the four-leaf clover springs open!

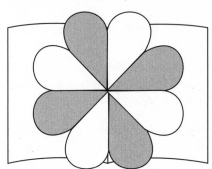

7 Decorate the front of the card with markers and crayons, paint, or glitter.

Variations

Have children experiment using other shapes to make different kinds of pop-up cards for occasions such as birthdays, Halloween, or April Fool's Day.

Festive Flowers

April showers bring May flowers. We know that spring is really here when we see daffodils, daisies, and tulips in bloom. Celebrate spring in your classroom by making a glorious bouquet of flowers.

 **Materials**

- painting supplies (see page 8)
- squares of brightly colored paper for flowers (an assortment of colors and sizes, from 3-inch to 6-inch squares)
- crayons
- scissors
- hole punch
- colored hole reinforcements (optional)
- pipe cleaners in assorted colors (the large, fuzzy ones work best)
- scraps of green paper (for leaves)

Getting Ready

Before starting this project, go outside for a flower-collecting field trip or bring some flowers into the classroom. (Some florists provide slightly aged flowers for educational purposes at no charge.) Help children to identify the parts of a flower (petal, stem, leaf, stamen, pistil). Compare different flower shapes. Some flowers have rounded petals, while others have pointy ones; some have just a few petals, some have many. Leaves come in many different shapes, too. Invite children to sketch some basic flower shapes before they make their paper flowers.

Hand out the materials and then show children how to do the following steps to make a basic flower.

Tip

This is the perfect project to start off by painting papers. Sponging, spattering, and combing are all well-suited techniques for patterning papers for these flowers. See pages 8–9 for how-to's. Allow papers to dry before going on to Step 1.

43

Tip

To make more natural-looking flowers and leaves, try curling and scoring them. See page 7 for how-to's.

1 Fold a piece of colored paper in half, then in half again.

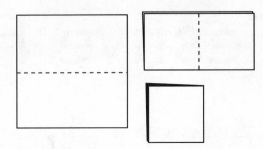

2 With a crayon, draw the shape of a petal on the folded paper. The shape should start on one of the folded edges and end on the other folded edge. Be sure not to draw all the way to the folded corner.

3 Cut out the shape and open the paper back up. This flower will have four petals. (For their next flower, have students try drawing two or three petals for a more complex, fuller flower.)

4 Use the hole punch to make a hole through the center of the flower. Decorate with colored hole reinforcements, if desired.

5 Push a pipe cleaner through the hole to make the flower's stem. Curl up the end above the hole so that the flower can't fall off. This will make the stamen. (For extra-strong stems, twist two pipe cleaners together.)

6 Cut leaf shapes out of green paper. Punch one or two holes at the base of each leaf and thread the stem through these holes.

Variations

◎ Make more complex flowers by layering two or three different sizes and shapes of petals on one stem. Work from the largest to the smallest as you thread them onto the stem.

◎ For daffodils, children can roll and glue a small piece of paper to form a tube. When the glue is dry, they can cut fringes at one end of the tube and roll the pieces back into curls. Then they can put glue on the other end of the tube and glue it to the center of a flower.

◎ For tulips, let children experiment making petals that they can turn upward and tape into place.

Ways to Display

Let these bright and colorful bouquets bloom all over your school! Invite children to create flower-filled vases (see page 46) to express their appreciation for important people in your school—for example, the maintenance staff, school secretaries, nurse, and bus drivers. These will also make wonderful gifts for other friends, as well as for family members.

Spring Flowers Vase

This unusual, beautiful, and easy-to-make container shows off the Festive Flowers children make on page 43.

Materials

For each student:

◎ one clean, empty soup can (with no rough edges)
◎ one 9- by 12-inch piece of colored construction paper (for covering can)
◎ one 9- by 12-inch piece of construction paper in a contrasting color

Other materials:

◎ 1-inch-wide ruler
◎ scissors
◎ tape

Pass out the materials. Then show the students how to do the following steps.

1 Wrap one piece of construction paper around the can and tape it in place. This will form a tube that is taller than the can. Add a bit of tape at the top of the tube. Also tape the paper to the can at the bottom, so it won't slip off.

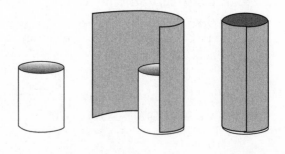

2 Fold the other piece of paper in half the long way as shown. Place a ruler along the long open edges and draw a line across the paper. Remove the ruler.

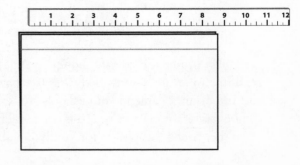

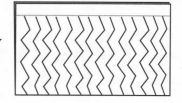

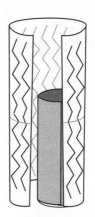

3 Make cuts from the folded edge all the way to the line. Do not cut past the line. Make a series of zigzag, wavy, or straight lines, about 1/2 inch apart.

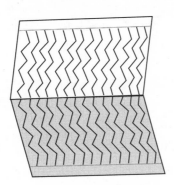

4 Carefully open up the paper. Wrap it around the can as shown and trim off any excess where the paper overlaps. Tape it in place. Once again, tape the paper to the bottom of the can so it won't slip off.

Tip

Before attaching the cut paper to the can, children can decorate it using any of the painting techniques described on pages 8–9.

5 The cut paper makes a tube that billows out in the middle where the paper was folded. Push the paper down until it is even with the top of the inner paper tube. Then fill with a bouquet of flowers!

Happy Earth Day Card

Celebrate Earth Day (April 22) or any spring occasion with this colorful card featuring a flower that blooms before your eyes! In the spirit of life and growth, attach a pretty seed packet to the card as an additional gift!

Materials

For each student:

- ◎ 1 large piece brightly colored construction paper, about 12 by 18 inches
- ◎ two 4-inch construction paper squares (same color or two different colors)
- ◎ 1 large paper fastener
- ◎ 1 green pipe cleaner
- ◎ 1 piece green construction paper
- ◎ seed packet (optional)

Other materials:

- ◎ scissors
- ◎ crayons or markers
- ◎ hole punch
- ◎ glue stick
- ◎ stapler

Pass out the materials. Then demonstrate for children the following steps.

1 Fold the large piece of paper in half twice as shown. Crease the folds with a thumb or the edge of a ruler. The folded edge will be the front of the card. (The double folds makes the card stronger.)

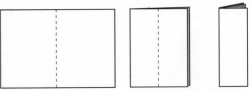

2 On the front of the card, write a message or make a drawing with crayons or markers. Then set the card aside.

3 Next, make the flower. Fold the two 4-inch paper squares in half as shown. Cut out a petal shape from each one, cutting through all layers of paper. Each folded piece of paper will make four petals.

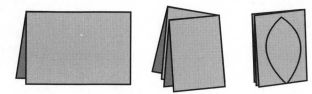

4 With a hole punch, make a hole in each petal near the base as shown.

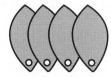

5 Push a paper fastener through the holes in the petals. If you are using two different colors of paper, try alternating them as you thread them onto the paper fastener.

6 Wrap about an inch of the pipe cleaner around the prongs of the fastener (behind the petals).

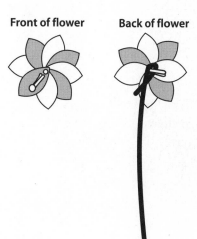

Front of flower   **Back of flower**

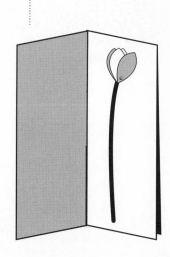

7 Place the flower on the right side of the open card. Push the paper fastener through the card and flatten the prongs in the back, as shown. Close up the petals so the flower looks like a bud. Staple the stem to the card near the bottom.

8 Cut some grass out of the green paper. Glue it to the bottom of the card so it covers the flower stem.

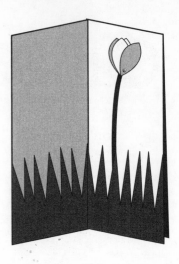

9 Optional: Glue the seed packet to the left-hand side of the open card in the open space, using spots of glue from a glue stick on the four back corners so it will be easy to detach later.

◎ This card will be a double surprise for a special relative or friend—the lucky recipient can spread open the petals to make the flower "bloom" and then plant the seeds in a window box or outside in a garden.

Quilt a Card

In this project, children make colorful quilts out of paper instead of cloth and thread. The interplay of patterns and colors and the visual rhyme created by the repetition of positive and negative shapes are a sure recipe for good design. These cards are perfect for Mother's Day, Father's Day, or any special occasion.

For each student:

- three 3-inch squares of construction paper (limit to 1 color, at least for the first time you do this activity)
- scissors
- 9- by 12-inch piece of construction paper (in a contrasting color)
- glue stick
- markers

Pass out the materials and demonstrate for children the following steps.

1 Fold the three-inch squares of paper in half. Cut shapes from the squares, beginning and ending your cut anywhere on the folded edge but staying clear of the open sides and corner (see diagram). Save both the shapes you cut out and the squares you cut them from. These are the quilt pieces that you will "appliqué" to your quilt. (Children may prefer to draw the shape on the paper instead of cutting it out freehand. Encourage them to make the three shapes different from one another.)

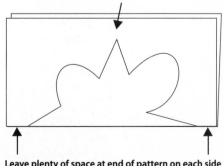

Leave plenty of space at end of pattern on each side and on top.

51

2 Fold the large piece of paper in half. This is the card that you will make your quilt on.

3 Glue one of the cutout squares onto the front of the card, lining it up in one corner.

4 Glue the other two cutout squares onto the card in checkerboard fashion with the squares touching at the corners.

5 Glue the last three cutout shapes in the remaining spaces on the card. It's not necessary to pair up the shapes with the squares they were cut from. In fact, it will be more interesting if you don't.

6 Write a greeting inside the card with markers or crayons.

Variations

PAINTED PATTERNS Before making the quilt card, paint patterns on the paper. (See About Painting, pages 8–9.) Bring in samples of patterned fabrics and invite children to use them as inspiration for their own designs. Children might also use squares of wrapping paper or other kinds of patterned paper for their cutout shapes.

TRICOLOR QUILT CARD Try using three different colors for the squares. Arrange the shapes and their squares so that the same colors are not right next to each other on the quilt.

Ways to Display

CLASS QUILT Have each student make a quilt, using six squares of construction paper and a 9- by 12-inch piece of construction paper (unfolded). Connect the squares by placing them facedown and side by side, then taping them together on the back.

STORY QUILT Give each class member a 9-inch square of paper. Use two contrasting colors for the squares. For example, if you have a class of 30 children, hand out 15 red and 15 yellow squares. Have children each make a scene on their square with scraps of paper. The scenes can be personal, about their family or pets, for example, or you may want to work the quilt into a theme for a unit you are currently working on. Then, place the squares facedown, side by side, in an alternating checkerboard pattern, and tape them together on the back.

Book Break

Let children get acquainted with the different types of traditional quilt designs and the history behind them.

Quilts: An American Heritage by Terri Zegart (Smithmark, 1994). This rich resource is filled with more than 130 color photos of different kinds of quilts.

Quilting Activities Across the Curriculum by Wendy Buchberg (Scholastic Professional Books, 1997). This innovative book includes folktales, writing prompts, patterning projects, literature selections, easy collaborative quilting projects, and a big, pullout poster of traditional quilt designs.

In *The Patchwork Quilt* by Valerie Flournoy (Dial, 1985), a young African American girl creates a quilt with the help of her grandmother.

The Keeping Quilt by Patricia Polacco (Simon & Schuster, 1988) describes the link provided by a quilt that is handed down through generations of a Jewish family.

Mini Bunny Piñata

I n Mexico children look forward to having a colorful piñata on their birthdays. Children will adore this adaptation of the traditional Mexican piñata. Instead of breaking it open, children pull on hanging pieces of yarn to release the goodies inside. For this project, let small groups of children work together to each make a piñata.

Materials

For each piñata:

- ◎ bunny patterns (page 78)
- ◎ two pieces of 9- by 12-inch white construction paper
- ◎ tape
- ◎ scissors
- ◎ markers
- ◎ paper hot drink cup with tight-fitting lid (not waxed, if possible)
- ◎ glue stick
- ◎ one piece of 9- by 12-inch pink construction paper
- ◎ large darning needle
- ◎ eight 12-inch pieces of yarn
- ◎ one 3-foot length of thick craft yarn
- ◎ wrapped candies and/or small toys to put inside the piñata

Pass out the materials. Then model for children the following steps.

1 Make the bunny's cheeks: Fold one piece of white construction paper in half the short way. Line up the bunny cheeks pattern box along the folded side of the construction paper. Tape the pattern to the paper to hold it in place during cutting. Cut out the cheeks and remove the pattern.

2 Using a marker, draw two front teeth and freckles or whiskers on the cheeks. (You may also paint the cup at this stage, if desired.)

3 Turn the paper cup upside down. Then glue the cheeks to the bottom edge of the cup so that the cheeks stick out on both sides.

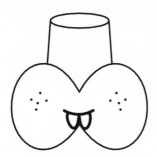

4 Make the ears: Glue together a piece of pink and a piece of white construction paper. When dry, fold the paper in half the long way. Tape the ear pattern box to the folded paper to hold it in place while cutting. Cut out the ear pattern to make two ears and remove the pattern.

5 Glue or tape the ears, with the white side facing out, to what is now the top of the cup, or the bunny's head. From the tip, make a fold, facing inward, about two inches down each ear—this will make the ears stand up straight!

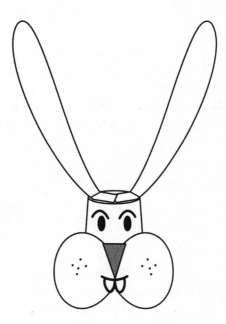

6 Cut out a pink nose from the scraps left over from the ears. Glue in place. Using markers, draw eyes for the rabbit on the cup.

Book Break

How did the piñata come to be? Children will enjoy the whimsical explanation in *Pancho's Piñata* by Stefan Czernecki and Timothy Rhodes (Hyperion, 1992).

Explore the land, culture, and customs of Mexico with *Culture Kit: Mexico* by Linda Scher and Mary Oates Johnson (Scholastic Professional Books, 1995). This complete theme unit on Mexico includes a map, a big colorful poster, activities, background information, and an audiocassette featuring folk songs and stories.

7 Thread the darning needle with one of the 12-inch pieces of yarn. Use the needle to punch a hole through the top of the lid. Pull the yarn through, until about one inch is sticking out from the bottom of the lid. Remove the needle. Then repeat this process with the other 7 pieces of yarn, being careful to evenly space the holes over the surface of the lid.

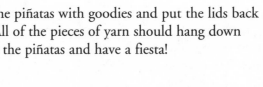

8 Make a double knot in one of the short ends of yarn. This is the only piece of yarn that will release the prizes when pulled. The other pieces of yarn will just pull off when tugged. Put the lid aside.

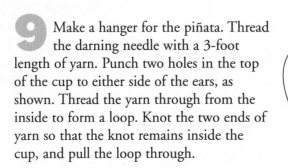

9 Make a hanger for the piñata. Thread the darning needle with a 3-foot length of yarn. Punch two holes in the top of the cup to either side of the ears, as shown. Thread the yarn through from the inside to form a loop. Knot the two ends of yarn so that the knot remains inside the cup, and pull the loop through.

10 Fill the piñatas with goodies and put the lids back on. All of the pieces of yarn should hang down freely. Hang up the piñatas and have a fiesta!

Variations

This piñata is in the form of a bunny, but with a little imagination your students are sure to dream up lots of ideas for different kinds of piñatas.

Ladybug, Ladybug

The ladybug or ladybird beetle is a favorite insect of many children and adults alike. Bright and perky-looking in their red jackets with black polka dots, ladybugs are a welcome, cheery sign of summer.

Materials

For each student:

- ladybug patterns (page 79)
- two 4-inch construction paper squares (one red, one black)
- black construction paper scraps
- 2 black pipe cleaners

Other materials:

- tape
- scissors
- hole punch
- glue

Pass out the materials and then demonstrate the following steps for children.

1 Fold the squares of construction paper in half. Line up the pattern boxes along the folded edge of the papers and tape them down in a few places. The wing pattern goes on the red paper and the body goes on the black paper.

2 Cut out the shapes along their outer edges, cutting through all layers of paper.

3 Using a hole punch, punch holes through the wings. These are the ladybug's spots. Remove the pattern. Open up the wings so that they angle upward.

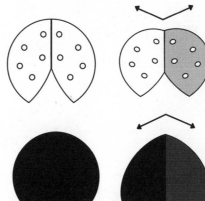

4 Remove the other pattern and open up the body so that it angles downward.

5 Attach the wings to the body with a small piece of tape or a dab of glue. If the wings or body flatten out as you work with them, simply reshape them after the tape is in place or the glue is dry. The wings should angle away from the body as if the ladybug is about to fly away home.

6 Cut out a head from a scrap of black construction paper and attach it to the front of the ladybug with a piece of tape.

7 Cut the pipe cleaners in half. Take three of the halves and twist them together in the middle to make the legs, as shown. Spread out the legs and form joints. Attach to the underside of the ladybug with tape or glue. For antennae, cut the last half pipe cleaner in half again and tape to the underside of the head. Trim and bend as desired.

Variations

◎ Students can easily make ladybug finger puppets by bending the legs of the ladybugs around their fingers.

◎ Invite children to adapt the basic ladybug design to make creepy crawlies such as spiders, grasshoppers, or other kinds of colorful beetles. Have books with pictures of different kinds of bugs on hand for children to look at. (See Book Break, left.)

Ways to Display

Celebrate ladybugs by setting them loose in your classroom. Invite students to place their ladybugs in different places around the room. How many can their classmates spot?

Flutter-By Butterfly

Summer is the time for playing out of doors and chasing fluttering butterflies as they do their very important work pollinating flowers. Children can add these colorful butterflies to the Festive Flowers they make (page 43).

Materials

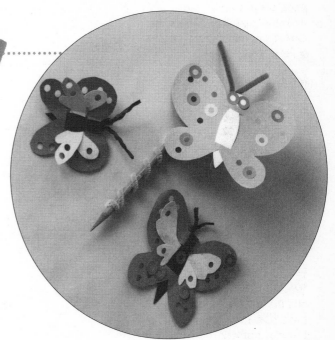

For each student:
- butterfly patterns (page 79)
- 1 piece colored construction paper, about 4-1/2 by 6 inches (for wings)
- 1 piece black or brown construction paper, about 2 by 6 inches (for body)
- scraps of colored paper (for decorating the wings)
- 1 pipe cleaner (the large, fuzzy kind works best)

Other materials:
- tape
- scissors
- paint, markers, crayons
- hole punch
- colored hole reinforcements (optional)
- glue stick

Pass out all supplies, including copies of the butterfly patterns. Have children cut out the butterfly pattern boxes. Then show them how to do the following steps.

1 Fold the pieces of construction paper in half. Line up the pattern boxes along the folded side of the papers as shown and tape down in a few places. The wings go on the larger paper and the body on the smaller paper.

 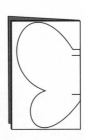

Book Break

Explore the beauty and majesty of butterflies with *The Butterfly Alphabet* by Kjell B. Sandved (Scholastic, 1996). This unusual book features spectacular close-up photos of butterfly wings, each revealing a pattern that resembles a letter in the alphabet from *A* to *Z*. Facing pages show how the entire butterfly looks.

Where Butterflies Grow by Joanne Ryder (Lodestar, 1989) lets young readers imagine what it feels like to change from a caterpillar into a black swallowtail butterfly. Lynne Cherry's meticulous and vibrant paintings complement the informative text.

2 Cut along the slots on the wing pattern, cutting through all layers of paper. Then cut out the wings, once again cutting through all layers of paper. Remove the pattern and open up the wings.

3 Decorate the wings with paints, markers, crayons, and scraps of paper; make holes with a hole punch; or add colored hole reinforcements.

4 Cut out the body, remove the pattern, and thread it through the slots in the wings. Draw a face on the butterfly's head.

5 Fold the pipe cleaner in half and bend the ends outward to look like antennae. Tape or glue to the back of the butterfly. Now your butterfly is ready to dip and dart away!

Variations

◎ Cut additional, smaller wing shapes out of paper and slip them under the butterfly's body. Try folding the wings up to look as though the butterfly has just alighted on a flower.

◎ Help children explore the symmetry in butterflies' wings. Share books that have pictures of butterflies. (See Book Break, page 60, for suggestions.) Then, after children cut out their butterfly's wings, let them experiment with painting designs on one wing, then pressing the two wings together to create a symmetrical effect.

Ways to Display

◎ Twist a second pipe cleaner around the middle of the antennae and use it to attach the butterfly to a paper flower.

◎ Twist the second pipe cleaner around a pencil to make a very special pencil topper—a butterfly that flutters as you write!

◎ Let children make buggy dioramas depicting an environment in which bugs might be found, perhaps a meadow, field, or backyard scene. Have them fill the scene with leaves, flowers, ladybugs, and butterflies that they make from paper.

Bookworm Bookmark and Reading Log

Encourage summer reading! Summer is the perfect time for kicking back and relaxing with a good book. This two-part project lets children make bookmarks to use all summer long and a log to keep a record of the books they read.

Materials

For each student:

- 1- by 12-inch strip of brightly colored construction paper
- 2 large paper clips (colored, if possible)
- two 4- by 18-inch strips of brightly colored construction paper

Other materials:

- scissors
- markers or crayons
- colored hole reinforcements (optional)
- glue

Bookworm Bookmark

Pass out the materials. Then show children how to do the following steps.

1 Use scissors to round off both ends of the 1- by 12-inch strip of paper. Starting at the end of the strip, make a fold about 1/2 to 3/4 inch deep. Then fold the paper back another 1/2 inch or so in the opposite direction. Keep folding back and forth until you have folded the entire piece of paper. This is called an accordion pleat.

2 Draw eyes on the bookworm or use hole reinforcements. (If you draw a line between the two circles it will look like the bookworm is wearing glasses!)

3 Using tape or ample glue, attach a paper clip to the back of the worm's head, letting the clip stick out about halfway. Let the glue dry completely.

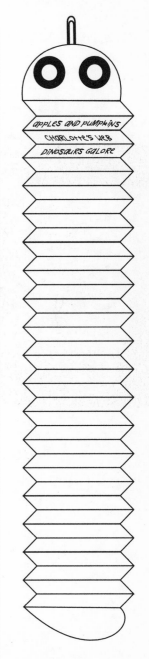

Bookworm Reading Log

1 Glue together the two 4- by 18-inch strips, end to end. Then make accordion pleats in the long strip as directed in step 1, making the folds about 1 inch apart.

2 Finish the bookworm log by following steps 2 and 3. A paper clip works as a hanger for the reading log.

3 Children can keep a record of each book they read by recording one title on each fold. The goal is to fill up the bookworm. Ambitious readers can turn the worm over and fill up the back. Encourage students to bring their bookworms back at the start of the new school year.

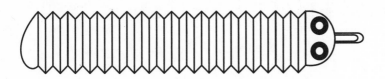
Variations

Have children experiment with pleating or fringing paper and using spattering, sponging, and other painting techniques to make other kinds of bookmark critters such as cats, dogs, snakes, or dragons.

Ways to Display

Create a Bookworm Bulletin Board in your classroom by posting students' reading logs. If possible, put a bookshelf under the board. Invite students to add to the log the title of each book they read, and encourage them to share book recommendations with their classmates. Place some of these recommended titles on the bookshelf for students to choose from.

Fancy Fans

Here's a cool and colorful way to keep cool on hot summer days. Fun and easy, children will want to make more than one of these fancy fans!

Materials

For each student:

◎ two 9- by 12-inch pieces of colored construction paper (the same color)

◎ one or two 3-foot lengths of colorful yarn

Other materials:

◎ scissors

◎ hole punch

◎ glue stick

Pass out the materials and show children how to do the following.

1 Make accordion folds (see page 62) about 1/2 inch to 3/4 inch wide along the short side of both pieces of the construction paper.

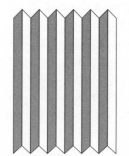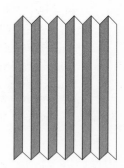

2 Cutting through one or two folds of the paper at a time, use scissors and a hole punch to cut simple shapes (squares or triangles, for example) out of the folded paper. About 2 inches from the bottom will be gathered together to make the handle, so you don't have to cut shapes all the way down.

3 Glue together the two pieces of paper at their folds so that they make a continuous accordion fold.

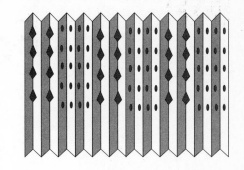

4 To make a handle, gather together the folds at the bottom of the fan. Then tie the yarn tightly around them about 2 inches up from the bottom, first in a knot, then in a bow. Or use more than one piece of different-colored yarns and tie on two bows for a really colorful effect!

5 Carefully spread open the fan as wide as you can. Fan-tastic!

Variations

◎ Instead of random shapes, cut a few pairs of slits close together into each fold, being careful not to cut all the way to the next fold. Poke the paper back through so that it folds in the opposite direction from the rest of the fold, as shown. This makes a really special three-dimensional fan that still creates a great breeze!

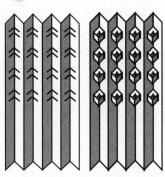

◎ Make a collage fan. Have children follow the directions above and then check their Scrap Savers (see page 11) for items to decorate their fans. Any leftover painted or patterned paper will look beautiful when glued onto the fans. Pieces of wrapping paper and magazine pages create unusual effects as well. Tell children to make the shapes small enough so that they don't wrap over the folds of the fan too much. To create a softer, looser look, encourage them to try tearing the paper instead of cutting it.

Ways to Display

Let students' fans become story prompts for creative writing. Tell students to pretend that their fans are magical. Have them write fantasy stories describing their fan's special powers and adventures with their fan. Display students' stories and fans on a Fantasy Fans Bulletin Board.

Summertime Journals

Children will love writing and making pictures in these summery journals. Directions are given for two different covers: Ocean Waves—a water scene with fish that look like they're underwater, and Sandy Shore—a beach scene covered with seashells and starfish half hidden in the sand. Of course, students can also come up with their own cover ideas.

Ocean Waves Cover

For each student:

◎ two 9- by 12-inch sheets of light blue construction paper (for front and back cover)
◎ one 9- by 12-inch sheet of construction paper (any other color)
◎ half of a small kitchen sponge

Sandy Shore Cover

For each student:

◎ two 9-by 12-inch sheets of yellow construction paper
◎ two 3-inch squares of yellow construction paper (for stencils)

Other materials:

◎ scissors
◎ plastic dishes filled with paint (blue and orange)
◎ old toothbrush
◎ hole punch
◎ glue stick
◎ water and paper towels for cleanup
◎ 1 yard of colored craft yarn (for each book)
◎ stack of 8 1/2- by 11-inch paper for inside of book, lined and unlined

Pass out the painting supplies, papers for the covers of the books, papers for stencils, and sponges, if children are making fish. Then show children how to do the following steps.

Making the Stencils and Stamps

🌀 **WAVE STENCIL:** Cut a wavy shape across the long
   edge of a 9- by 12-inch piece of paper.

🌀 **STARFISH AND SEASHELL STENCILS:** Cut simple
   seashell and star shapes out of the 3-inch
   yellow paper squares.

🌀 **FISH STAMP:** Cut a simple fish shape out of the
   sponge.

Painting the Designs

🌀 **FISH:** Wet the sponge and wring it out well. Then press the sponge into
   orange paint, coating the entire surface. Use the sponge as a stamp, pressing
   it down firmly on the light blue paper. You'll probably be able to make two
   or three stamps out of each spongeful of paint. Tilt the fish at different
   angles or make them go in one direction like a school of fish. Stamp both
   pieces of light blue paper. Allow fish to dry.

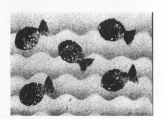

🌀 **WAVES:** Place the wave stencil on the same paper you stamped the fish on, positioning the stencil about 2 inches from the top of the paper. Using the spattering technique (see page 8), spatter the paper with a toothbrush lightly coated with dark blue paint. Try to direct the paint so that it builds up along the edge of the stencil. Now move the stencil down another 2 inches and repeat. Continue this process until you've spattered the whole page. Let the paper dry.

🌀 **SANDY SHORE:** Place the seashell and starfish shapes on a piece of yellow paper. Using orange paint, spatter around the shapes, being sure to get all the edges. Fill your toothbrush lightly and keep refilling it as needed. Now pick up the stencil shapes and move them to a different spot on the paper, turning the shapes at different angles to make the composition

more interesting. Repeat spattering. Keep moving the stencils around and spattering until you are pleased with the results. Don't forget the edges of the paper! Repeat this process with the other sheet of yellow paper. Let the papers and stencils dry. The stenciled shapes on the paper will look like seashells hidden in the sand! The two stencils can be glued to the front cover to look like seashells sitting on top of the sand.

Making the Journal

1 Insert a stack of plain paper between the front and back covers. If you like, alternate lined and white paper for writing and drawing.

2 Using a hole punch, punch four holes through the left-hand side of the stack of papers. (Do this in batches, using the first page as a template, if the stack is too thick.) Make sure all the holes line up.

3 Thread the yarn through the top and bottom holes as shown. Pull the ends to the back of the book until they are even. Now bring the ends back up through the center holes. Tie them first in a knot and then a bow. Cut off ends to the desired length.

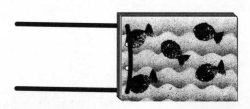

Collages for All Seasons

Collage is a great technique, not only as a way to use up leftover materials but as a very fun, free, and easy way to make a picture. Use construction paper, wrapping papers, candy wrappers, magazine or newspaper pages, or anything else!

Materials

For each student:

- 9- by 12-inch piece of construction paper, or larger (to back collage)
- paper scraps
- scissors
- glue stick

Pass out all supplies. Encourage students to look at their scraps to see if they suggest an idea for something. Or they can start with an idea and cut the scraps to make them work. Then guide students through the following steps.

1 On the backing paper, arrange scraps until you like the way your picture looks. Cut out any shapes you need to finish your picture. It may take some experimenting and playing around to find the best *composition* (the way you place things on the page). Remember that it's fine to overlap the papers.

2 Think about *contrast*—colors and how they look together. Some colors make each other look stronger and are easy to see when they are side by side—yellow and red, for instance. Other colors are harder to see next to each other—for instance, yellow and light blue or blue and purple. Think about the contrast when you put down a shape. If you have trouble seeing a shape, you may need to change its color or position.

3 When you are happy with your picture, it's time to glue the pieces down. But don't remove all the pieces at once because you won't remember where you wanted to put them! Using a glue stick, remove one piece from your composition at a time. Apply glue to the back, working on a piece of scrap paper. Then return the glued scrap to your picture in the place where it belongs. Keep gluing until all the pieces of your collage are secured. Allow to dry completely.

Variations

- Try making a picture using only geometric shapes—triangles, circles, rectangles, or squares.
- A picture that is made with lots of little squares is called a mosaic. If your class would like to try making a mosaic, pass out sheets of large graph paper. Precut squares to the size of the graph squares in different colors.

Ways to Display

Students may enjoy including poems in their collages or cutting a frame out of the collage to put around a picture.

Frisky Fall Squirrel • Body

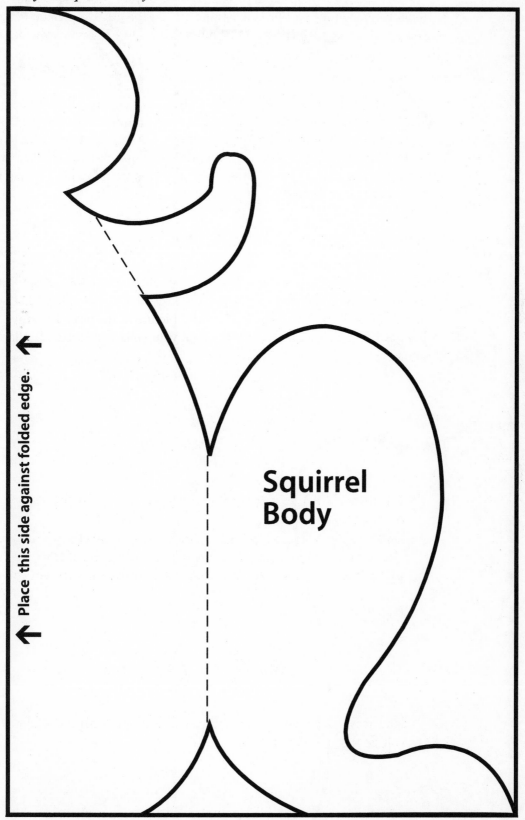

Place this side against folded edge.

Squirrel Body

Frisky Fall Squirrel • *Tail*

Frisky Fall Squirrel • *Head*

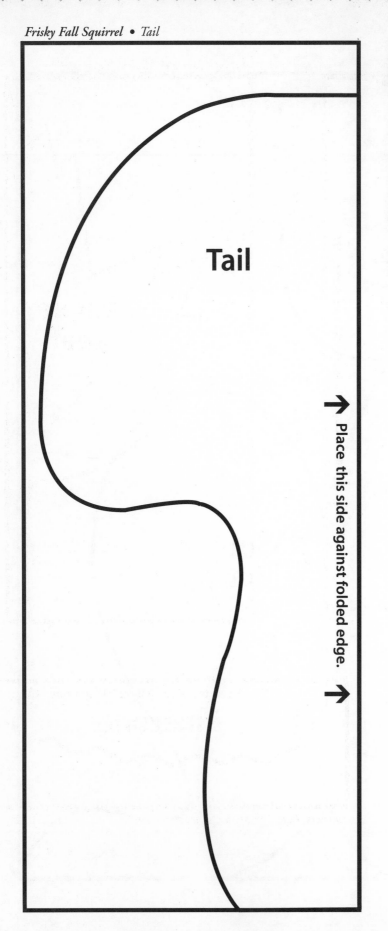

Tail

Place this side against folded edge.

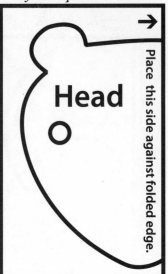

Head

Place this side against folded edge.

Autumn Leaves & More • Oak Leaf

Oak Leaf

Place this side against folded edge. →

Autumn Leaves & More • Maple Leaf

Maple Leaf

Place this side against folded edge. →

Acorn

Place this side along folded edge.

Autumn Leaves & More • Acorn

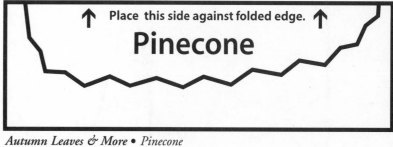

↑ Place this side against folded edge. ↑

Pinecone

Autumn Leaves & More • Pinecone

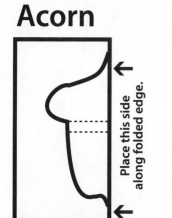

Going Batty • Bat Wings & Body

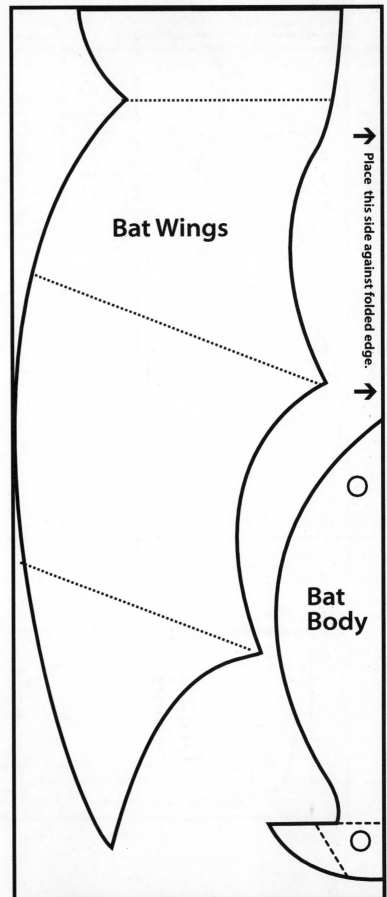

Bat Wings

Place this side against folded edge.

Bat Body

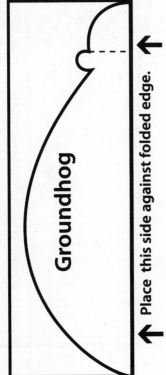

Groundhog Pop-Up Card • Groundhog

Groundhog

Place this side against folded edge.

74

Perky Turkey • *Turkey*

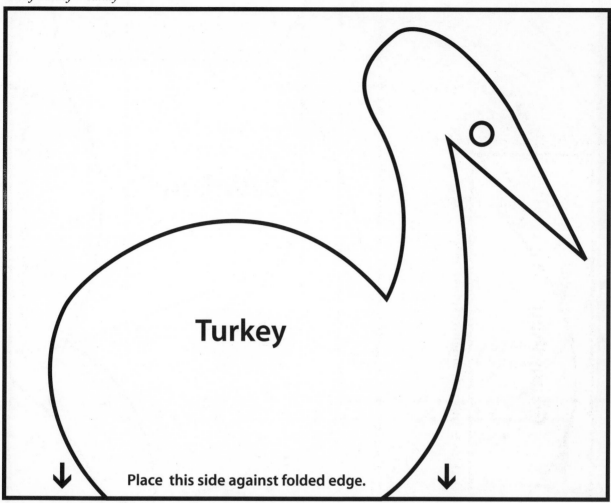

Turkey

Place this side against folded edge.

Chinese New Year's Dragon • *Head*

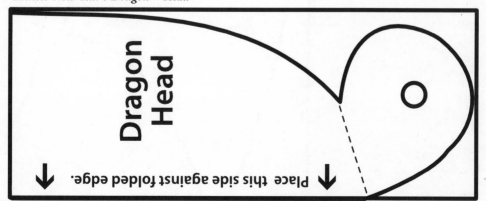

Dragon Head

Place this side against folded edge.

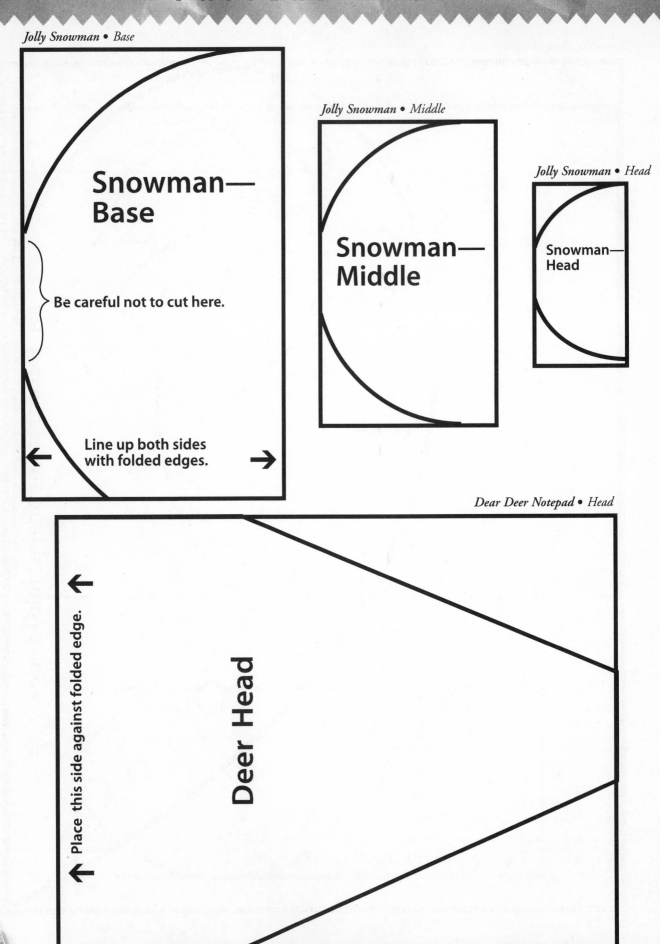

Jolly Snowman • Base

Snowman—Base

Be careful not to cut here.

Line up both sides with folded edges.

Jolly Snowman • Middle

Snowman—Middle

Jolly Snowman • Head

Snowman—Head

Dear Deer Notepad • Head

Deer Head

Place this side against folded edge.

Valentine Keeper • Heart

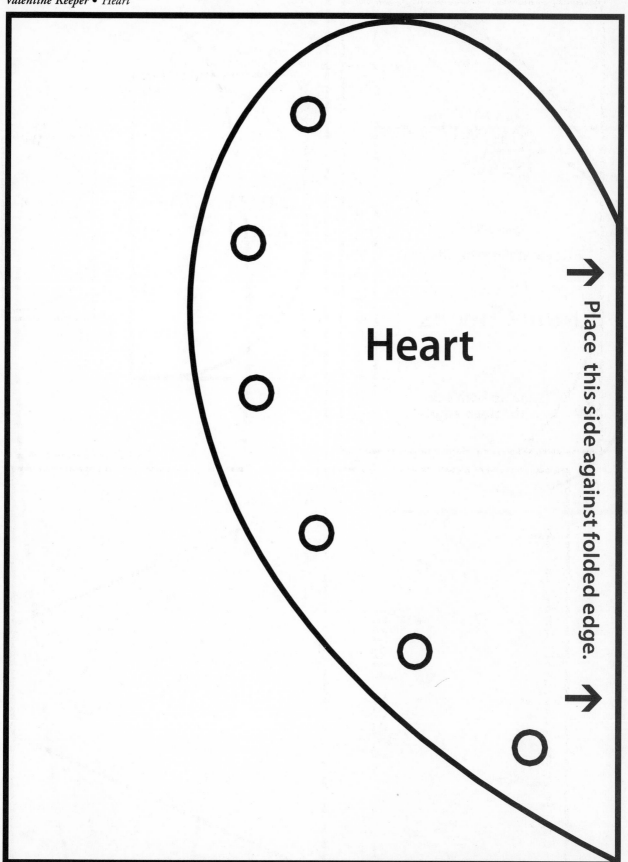

Heart

Place this side against folded edge.

Mini Bunny Piñata • Ears

Mini Bunny Piñata • Cheeks

Bunny Cheeks

Place this side against folded edge.

Bunny Ears

78

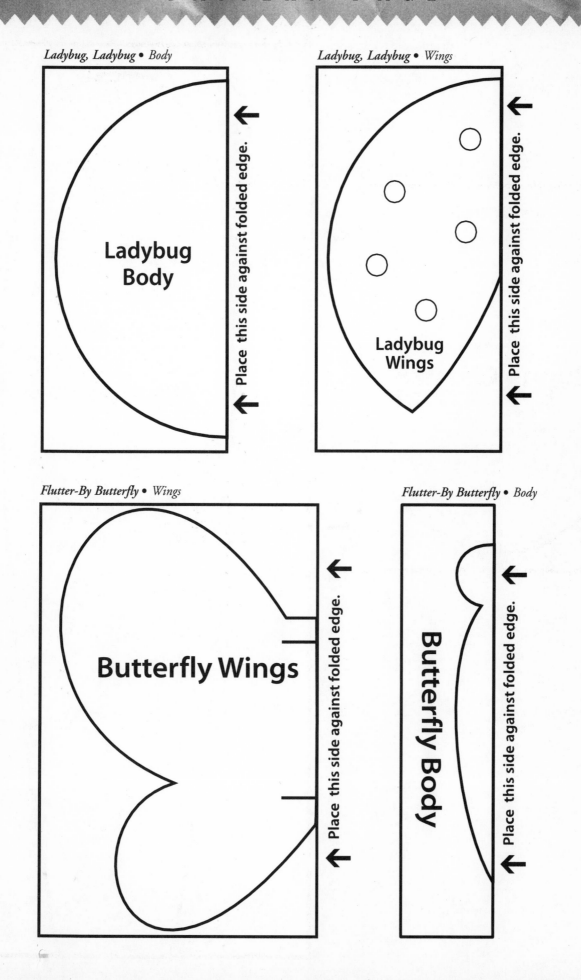

Ladybug, Ladybug • Body

Ladybug Body

Place this side against folded edge.

Ladybug, Ladybug • Wings

Ladybug Wings

Place this side against folded edge.

Flutter-By Butterfly • Wings

Butterfly Wings

Place this side against folded edge.

Flutter-By Butterfly • Body

Butterfly Body

Place this side against folded edge.